Shine On! Plus 5

Workbook

T0346909

Contents

OXFORD
UNIVERSITY PRESS

Welcome!

1 Find and circle the months of the year. Write in order.

o	m	i	d	l	a	u	g	u	s	t
c	a	t	e	j	u	l	y	c	q	s
t	r	a	c	b	d	j	u	n	e	e
o	c	k	e	x	j	m	s	o	w	p
b	h	n	m	v	a	z	b	v	r	t
e	g	y	b	f	n	a	h	e	j	e
r	z	r	e	n	u	p	b	m	t	m
f	e	b	r	u	a	r	y	b	u	b
c	b	v	s	q	r	i	h	e	l	e
p	m	a	y	l	y	l	w	r	c	r

1 <u>January</u>   7 _____

2 _____   8 _____

3 _____   9 _____

4 _____   10 _____

5 _____   11 _____

6 _____   12 _____

2 Read. Write questions and answers.

① Maya   **June 6**

When is Maya's birthday?
Maya's birthday is in June.

② Tim   **March 18**

_____
_____

③ Kai   **August 10**

_____
_____

④ Sofia   **January 30**

_____
_____

Vocabulary Months of the year **Grammar** When is Maya's birthday? Maya's birthday is in June.

1 Look, read, and write.

Charlie's birthday is in March.   When is Stella's birthday?
~~This new smartboard is cool!~~   Stella's birthday is in September.
Lily's birthday is in May!   I can't read it.

①

This new smartboard is cool!

②

January, February, March …

Look! There you are, Charlie!

③

When is Lily's birthday?
_____

And my birthday is in July!

④

_____

Touch September!

⑤

Oh, what's that?

_____
What is it, Amy?   I don't know.

⑥

It's another puzzle!

How exciting!

OK, Junior Crew! Let's go!

2 Read and answer.

When is Joe's birthday? _____

A Special Concert

Lesson 1 **Story: The Big Band**

1 Order the story. Read and circle.

It's time for the **party / parade**!

Let's go!

Hi, **Uncle / Aunt** May? We need your help. Can you come to the parade?

Yes / No, of course!

One, two, **thirteen / three**! All together!

What are you **playing / doing**, Aunt May?

I'm playing the drums. I'm playing the xylophone. And I'm playing the **violin / guitar**!

Our instruments are on the **bus / train**! My drums!

My guitar!

My xylophone!

Hi! What are you playing?

I'm playing the **trumpet / flute**.

I'm playing the violin.

1 Complete the puzzle. Match.

■	❀	◎	✖	⬚	▲	◗	➤	▣	◆	✳	✳	○	✛	☆	⬟	▢	✴	◉	✧	♥	◈	●	▴	✳	★
a	b	c	d	e	f	g	h	i	j	k	l	m	n	o	p	q	r	s	t	u	v	w	x	y	z

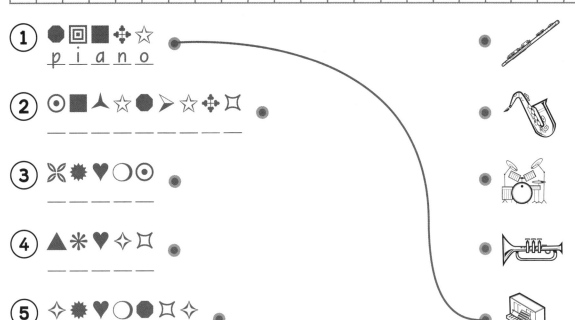

① ●▣■✛☆
<u>p</u> <u>i</u> <u>a</u> <u>n</u> <u>o</u>

② ◉■▴☆●➤☆✛⬚
_ _ _ _ _ _ _ _ _

③ ✖✴♥○◉
_ _ _ _ _

④ ▲✳♥✧⬚
_ _ _ _ _

⑤ ✧✴♥○●⬚✧
_ _ _ _ _ _ _

2 Look, read, and match.

 Adam   Maria   Aliya   Omar

1 What are you playing, Aliya? ●   ● I'm playing the violin.

2 What are you playing, Adam? ●   ● I'm playing the xylophone.

3 What are you playing, Omar? ●   ● I'm playing the saxophone.

4 What are you playing, Maria? ●   ● I'm playing the guitar.

Vocabulary Musical instruments **Grammar** What are you playing? I'm playing the piano.

1 Lesson 3

1 Look, read, and circle.

①

Are they playing table tennis?

Yes, they are. / No, they aren't.

②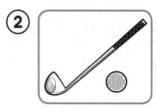

Are they playing golf?

Yes, they are. / No, they aren't.

③

Are they playing ice hockey?

Yes, they are. / No, they aren't.

④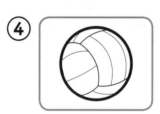

Are they playing volleyball?

Yes, they are. / No, they aren't.

2 Write the words in order to make questions and answers.

①

are. they golf? Yes, Are they playing

Are they playing golf?
Yes, they are.

②

they table tennis? they No, aren't. Are playing

_____
_____

③

Yes, playing they are. they volleyball? Are

_____
_____

④

aren't. Are ice hockey? playing No, they they

_____
_____

Vocabulary Sports **Grammar** Are they playing table tennis? Yes / No, they are / aren't.

1 Follow, read, and write.

conductor   percussion   brass   woodwind   strings

1 _____

2 _____

3 _____

4 _____

5 _____

2 Read, circle, and draw.

①

Sara: Guess the instrument!
Pedro: Does it have strings?
Sara: No.
Pedro: Do you play it with your mouth?
Sara: Yes.
Pedro: It's a **guitar** / **saxophone**.

②

Tom: Guess the instrument!
Olivia: Is it made of metal?
Tom: Yes.
Olivia: Is it in the brass family?
Tom: No.
Olivia: It's a **flute** / **trumpet**.

1   Look, read, and write.

Yes   fun   Can   play   course

That looks _____ .
_____ I _____ , too?

_____ , of _____ .

2   Look, read, and write *Maria* or *Diego*.

1   __Diego__ : I'm playing golf.

2   _____ : That looks fun. Can I play, too?

3   _____ : Yes, of course.

4   _____ : That looks fun. Can I play, too?

5   _____ : Yes, of course.

6   _____ : That looks fun. Can we play, too?

7   _____ : Sorry, no thanks!

1 Read, choose, and write.

①

James

I'm at the _____. There are many sports teams here. People are playing soccer, table tennis, and basketball. I'm playing ice hockey. My ice hockey team is great!

②

Tanya

I'm at the _____. There are many people here. They're very happy. You can dance here. There's a band. They're playing the drums and the trumpet. It's great!

③

Evie

I'm at the _____. There are many fun things to do. People are playing volleyball. People are playing in the ocean. I'm playing the guitar. We can eat ice cream. It's a great day!

2 Look at activity 1. Read and circle.

1 James, what are you playing?
I'm playing **table tennis / ice hockey**.

2 Evie, what are you playing?
I'm playing the **flute / guitar**.

3 Tanya, what are people playing at the town parade?
They're playing the **drums and the trumpet / drums and the violin**.

4 James, what are people playing at the sports competition?
They're playing **soccer and table tennis / golf and volleyball**.

International Day

Lesson 1 | **Story: Everybody Likes Pizza!**

1 Look, read, and write.

> We like pizza!   I'm hungry.
> Where are you from?   We're from Australia.

① Let's talk to people from all the countries. _____

Look! There's Italy. They have pizza on their table!

② Where are you from?

We're from Brazil!

_____

③ Hi! Where are you from?

_____

We like pizza, too!

④ _____

We're from Japan.

That's cool! Can we take a photo for the magazine?

2 Find and write *Yes, they are.* or *No, they aren't.*

① Are they from Australia? _____

② Are they from Japan? _____

③ Are they from Brazil? _____

④ Are they from Italy? _____

1 Look, read, and number.

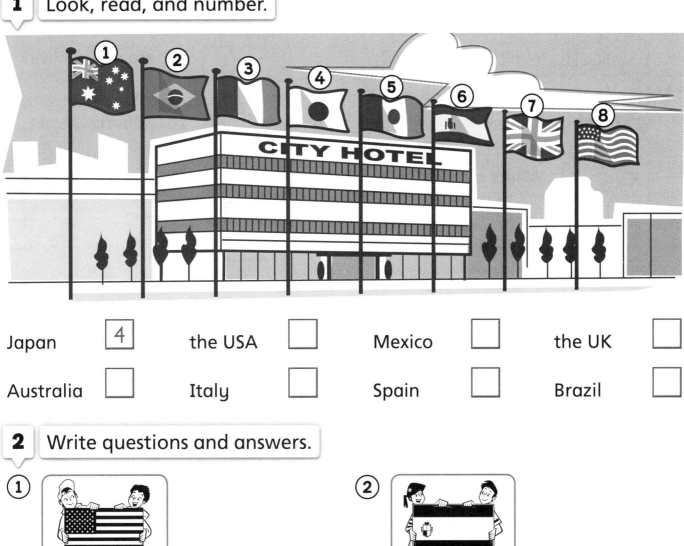

| Japan | 4 | the USA | ☐ | Mexico | ☐ | the UK | ☐ |
| Australia | ☐ | Italy | ☐ | Spain | ☐ | Brazil | ☐ |

2 Write questions and answers.

①

Where are you from?
We're from the USA.

②

③

④

1 Look, read, and make a ✓ or an ✗.

① Where do you live?

I live in a city. ☐

② Where do you live?

I live in the suburbs. ☐

③ Where do you live?

I live in the countryside. ☐

④ Where do you live?

I live in a town. ☐

2 Look, read, and write.

> I live in a town.   Where do you live?
> I'm from Japan.   Where are you from?

① Where are you from?

_____

_____

I live in a city.

② _____

I'm from the USA.

Where do you live?

_____

2 Lesson 4 Geography

1 Look, read, and match.

①  ②  ③  ④

tower   building   monument   statue

2 Look, read, and write.

¹ Australia

Capital city: Canberra

Famous ² _____ : Sydney Opera House

Famous monument: Sydney Harbour Bridge

Famous ³ _____ : Sydney Tower

Interesting Fact:
Sydney Tower is 309 meters tall!

Sydney Opera House
Sydney Harbour Bridge

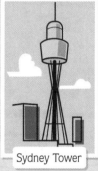
Sydney Tower

4 _____

Capital city: Mexico City

Famous building: Museo Soumaya

Famous ⁵ _____ : Angel of Independence

Famous ⁶ _____ : Teotihuacan

Interesting Fact: There are more than 66,000 pieces of art in Museo Soumaya.

Museo Soumaya

Angel of Independence

Teotihuacan

1 Look, read, and write.

Pleased to meet you, too.   I'm from the USA.
Hi, pleased to meet you!   Where are you from?

Where are you from?

I'm from Mexico.

2 Look, read, and number in order.

Glad to meet you, Lucas. I'm Haru. ☐

Hello! I'm Lucas. 1

Yes, of course. Here you are, Lucas! ☐

That looks fun. Can I play, too? ☐

I'm playing table tennis. ☐

I'm from Japan. ☐

I'm from Brazil. Where are you from? ☐

Where are you from, Lucas? ☐

2 Lesson 6

1 Read and circle.

1 **Ben:** Hi, what's your name?
  Mia: A Nice to meet you.
      B My name's Mia.
      C I'm from Mexico.

2 **Ben:** I'm Ben. Pleased to meet you.
  Mia: A Pleased to meet you, too.
      B I live in Mexico City.
      C My name's Mia.

3 **Ben:** Where are you from?
  Mia: A Mexico is quite big.
      B I'm from Mexico.
      C I live in a city.

4 **Mia:** Where are you from?
  Ben: A I'm from Australia.
      B Australia is great!
      C I live in the suburbs.

5 **Ben:** Where do you live in Mexico?
  Mia: A Mexico is very nice.
      B I live in Mexico City.
      C Mexico City is the capital
         of Mexico.

6 **Mia:** Where do you live?
  Ben: A Australia is a big country.
      B Canberra is the capital of
         Australia.
      C I live in the countryside.

2 Read and answer for you.

Mia: Hi, what's your name?

You: 1 _____

Mia: I'm Mia. Nice to meet you.

You: 2 _____

Mia: Where are you from?

You: 3 _____

Mia: Where do you live?

You: 4 _____

Mia: I'm from Mexico. Here, this is a
     taco, from Mexico.

You: Thank you, Mia!

Revision 1

1 Look, read, and number.

 ☐  ☐  ☐ 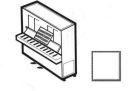 ☐

 ☐ 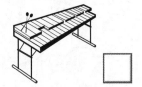 ☐  ☐  ☐

1 piano   **2** guitar   **3** drums   **4** saxophone

5 violin   **6** trumpet   **7** xylophone   **8** flute

2 Look, draw, and write.

①    Spain

②   _____

③   _____

④      _____

⑤      _____

⑥      _____

⑦   _____

⑧   _____

3 Write the words in order to make questions and answers. Look and number.

1 I you suburbs. do in live live? the Where

_____

_____

3 Japan. are Where from? from We're you

_____

_____

2 playing saxophone. are playing? you the What I'm

_____

_____

4 playing Yes, they Are are. they table tennis?

_____

_____

4 Read and match.

1 What are you playing?   ●

2 Are they playing
   ice hockey?   ●

3 Where are you from?   ●

4 Are they playing the piano?   ●

5 Where do you live?   ●

6 What are they playing?   ●

● No, they aren't. They're playing volleyball.

● They're playing the drums.

● Yes, they are.

● We're from the USA.

● I'm playing the violin.

● I live in the countryside.

The New Store

Lesson 1 | **Story: A Great Present!**

1 Look, read, and make a ✓ or an ✗.

The electronics store is new. ☐

It's Charlie's birthday. ☐

Joe wants a camera. ☐

He doesn't want a watch. ☐

The present is a tablet. ☐

He likes the present. ☐

2 Read and circle.

Joe's birthday is in **June / July**.

18

1 | Look, unscramble, and write.

① l e c l   h e o p n

cell   _phone_

②  r a e a c m

_____

③  m g a s e   l c n o o s e

_____   _____

④ l a r t o l c u c a

_____

⑤ V T

_____

⑥  a t p l p o

_____

⑦ b a l t t e

_____

⑧ d n p e a s h e o h

_____

2 | Follow and write.

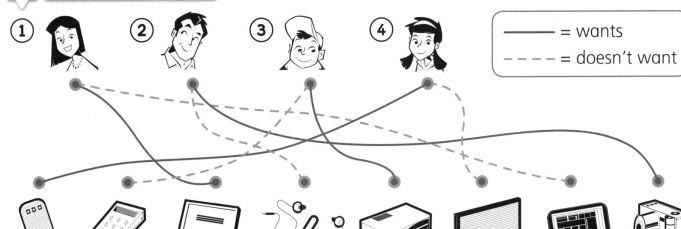

———— = wants
– – – – = doesn't want

1 She wants a laptop.   She doesn't want a tablet.

2 _____   _____

3 _____   _____

4 _____   _____

1 Look, read, and circle.

①

What do they want?

They **want / don't want** watchbands.

②

What do they want?

They **want / don't want** laptop cases.

③

What does he want?

He **wants / doesn't want** a camera bag.

④

What does she want?

She **wants / doesn't want** a cell phone cover.

2 Write questions and answers.

 **Max** 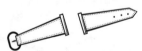 **Leo and Sofia**  **Lucia**   **Dan and Pete**

1 Lucia

<u> What does she want? </u>

_____

2 Leo and Sofia

_____

_____

3 Max

_____

_____

4 Dan and Pete

_____

_____

Vocabulary Accessories **Grammar** What do they want? They want laptop cases.

3 **Lesson 4** **Computing**

1 Look, read, and write.

shop online   watch videos
chat with friends   learn things

①    ②    ③    ④

_____   _____   _____   _____

_____

2 Look, read, and circle *True* or *False*.

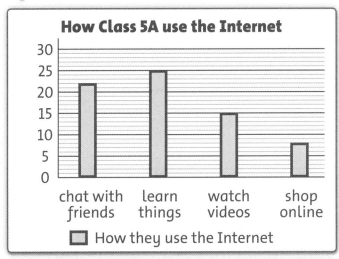

How Class 5A use the Internet

How they use the Internet

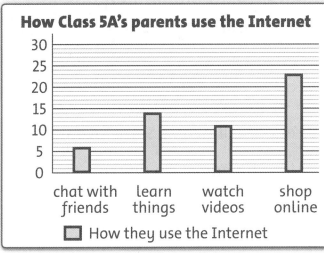

How Class 5A's parents use the Internet

How they use the Internet

1 22 children chat with friends.
True / False

2 23 parents shop online.
True / False

3 15 parents watch videos.
True / False

4 14 children learn things.
True / False

5 8 children shop online.
True / False

6 6 parents chat with friends.
True / False

7 11 children watch videos.
True / False

8 8 parents shop online.
True / False

Vocabulary use the Internet, shop online, watch videos, chat with friends, learn things

1 Look, read, and match.

No, not really.

Yes, I like it a lot.

I like this cell phone cover. Do you?

2 Look, read, and number.

1 Yes, of course.

2 Hi David. What are you playing?

3 I'm playing this new game.

4 That looks fun. Can I play, too?

1 Yes, I like it a lot. It's my favorite!

2 I like this game. Do you?

3 Lesson 6

1 Look, read, and match.

①

Digital World

Digital World is a great place to shop for any computer or tablet! What computer or tablet do you want? You can find it at Digital World! You can shop for laptop cases, too!

Emma

②

Perfect Pics

You can shop for big cameras or small cameras at **Perfect Pics**. **Perfect Pics** is a great place to shop for camera bags, too.

Shop at Perfect Pics online today!

Daisy

③

Fantastic Phones

Use your computer to go to Fantastic Phones online. Or you can shop for cell phones in our store. Look at all our cell phones and cell phone covers! Find a fantastic phone today!

Nick

④

Great Games

Do you like computer games?

Then come to Great Games! You can buy a games console and many great computer games. What game do you want? You can find it at Great Games!

Dan   Pete

2 Look at activity 1. Read and write.

1 What does Emma want?   She wants a _____.

2 What can you shop for at Digital World?   _____

3 What do Dan and Pete want?   _____

4 What store can you shop at online?   _____

5 What store does Nick want?   _____

6 What can you shop for at Perfect Pics?   _____

Big Numbers

Lesson 1 | **Story: My Favorite Player!**

1 Order the story.

2 Circle the numbers in the story.

2 3 7 8 20 21 22 23 35 36 37 61 62 63 99 100

4 Lesson 2

1 Read and circle. Write.

① (thirty) **30** forty

    thirty

② sixty **40** forty

③ fifty **50** twenty

④ one hundred **60** sixty

⑤ fifty **70** seventy

⑥ sixty **80** eighty

⑦ ninety **90** thirty

⑧ one hundred **100** ninety

2 Look and write questions and answers.

① How much is this?  **$38**   It's thirty-eight dollars.

② _____  **$42** _____

③ _____  **$56** _____

④ _____  **$100** _____

⑤ _____  **$77** _____

⑥ _____ **$86** _____

1 Look and read. Write and circle.

① How many pencils are there?
There are ___thirty-six___ pencils in the (box)/ jar.

② How many potatoes are in there?
There are _____ potatoes in the **bunch** / **bag**.

③ How many olives are there?
There are _____ olives in the **box** / **jar**.

④ How many balloons are there?
There are _____ balloons in the **bunch** / **bag**.

2 Write the words in order to make questions. Write the answers.

24 potatoes   15 eggs   5 flowers

1 there? eggs many How are

_____   _____

2 many are there? How potatoes

_____   _____

3 flowers many there? How are

_____   _____

Vocabulary Countable foods and objects **Grammar** How many pencils are there? There are thirty-six pencils.

4 Lesson 4 | Math

1 Look, unscramble, and write.

① − ⓝ ⓜ ⓘ ⓢ ⓤ _____

② ✕ ⓜ ⓔ ⓣ ⓘ ⓢ _____

③ ✚ ⓛ ⓤ ⓟ ⓢ _____

④ ÷ ⓘ ⓓ ⓓ ⓘ ⓓ ⓔ ⓥ ⓨ ⓑ _____

⑤ ═ ⓠ ⓐ ⓤ ⓔ ⓢ ⓛ _____

2 Read and write the sums.

It's Anna's birthday! Anna and her family are at her birthday picnic.

1 Anna gets three bunches of balloons. There are eight balloons in a bunch. How many balloons are there?

8 x 3 = _____

2 There are twenty-two children at the picnic. There are twelve parents at the picnic. How many people are there at the picnic?

22 _____

3 There are forty sandwiches. People eat twenty-eight sandwiches. How many sandwiches are there now?

40 _____

4 There are forty-four cakes. There are twenty-two children at the picnic. How many cakes do they get?

44 _____

Vocabulary plus, minus, times, divided by, equals   27

1 Look, read, and circle.

Which one do you **want** / **get**?

I want the **old** / **small** one, **please** / **thank you**.

2 Look, read, and write.

really   please   like   want   No   you   Which

I _____ this one. Do _____ ?

_____ , not _____ . It's very big and heavy.

_____ one do you _____ ?

I want the long one, _____ .

4 Lesson 6

1 Read and write the sums.

①

Name: Jago Jones

Age: twenty-nine years old

Sport: soccer

Favorite food: olives

Interesting Fact: Jago can eat one jar of olives every week! He runs for forty-five minutes in the morning and twenty-five minutes in the afternoon.

How many minutes does Jago run for?   45 + 25 = _____

②

Name: Lina Smith

Age: twenty-five years old

Sport: volleyball

Favorite food: oranges

Interesting Fact: There are sixty-five bags of oranges at the volleyball games. Lina and her team eat twelve bags of oranges after the game!

How many bags of oranges are there for the other volleyball players?   _____

③

Name: Dylan Green

Age: thirty-one years old

Sport: ice hockey

Favorite food: bananas

Interesting Fact: Dylan eats three bunches of bananas every week. There are six bananas in each bunch!

How many bananas does Dylan eat?   _____

2 Look at activity 1. Read and write.

1 Who is number thirty-two?   _____

2 Who is thirty-one years old?   _____

3 Who likes olives?   _____

4 Who is twenty-five years old?   _____

5 Who is number fifty-seven?   _____

6 Who likes bananas?   _____

Revision 2

1 Read, look, and write. Find the hidden word.

Letter 1 is in <u>calculator</u> , _____ , and **30** _____ .

Letter 2 is in _____ , _____ , and _____ .

Letter 3 is in _____ of apples, _____ ,
and _____ of bananas.

Letter 4 is in _____ , _____ , and **11** _____ .

Letter 5 is in _____ , **35** _____ , and **72** _____ .

Letter 6 is in box of _____ , _____ ,
and _____ .

The hidden word is __ __ <u>b</u> __ __ __ .
                1 2 3 4 5 6

2 Look and number in order. Write.

72	38	54	96	49	83	100	65
☐	1	☐	☐	☐	☐	☐	☐

1 <u>thirty-eight</u>   2 _____   3 _____   4 _____

5 _____   6 _____   7 _____   8 _____

3 Read, look, and answer. Write *Store 1* or *Store 2*.

1 **Pixons**
We sell cameras, TVs, and games consoles! Do you need a camera bag or a watchband? Come to Pixons!

2 **Compulse**
Do you need a new laptop? Or a laptop case? Do you want a tablet? Come to Compulse! We sell headphones and calculators, too.

① What does she want?

She wants _____ . She doesn't want a _____ .
Store 1

② What do they want?

_____ . _____ .
_____

③ What does he want?

_____ . _____ .
_____

4 Read the questions and answers. Look and write correct answers.

1 How many chocolates are in the box?
There are ~~twenty-six~~ chocolates in the box.
There are twenty-two chocolates in the box.

2 How many peaches are in the bag?
There are ~~thirty-two~~ peaches in the bag.
_____

3 How much is the jar of olives?
It's ~~ninety-two~~ cents.
_____

4 How much is the bunch of flowers? It's ~~forty-six~~ dollars.
_____

5 A Busy Day

Lesson 1 **Story: A Famous Singer in Town**

1 Look, read, and write.

She gets up at eight o'clock. She plays with her friends at four thirty. She's making a music video. What time does she go to school?

①

Nicky News is in town!

_____
_____

Let's go and meet her!

②

Nicky is asleep.

What time does she get up?

_____

③

_____
_____

Nicky isn't going to school today. Her teacher is coming to the hotel.

④

She does her homework at three o'clock. _____
_____

You can play too!

2 Read and number in order.

☐ The Junior Crew meet Nicky News.

☐ The Junior Crew sing a song with Nicky News.

☐ The Junior Crew go to the hotel. Nicky News is asleep.

1 The Junior Crew see Nicky News on TV.

1 Look, read, and match.

1 get — my homework

2 get — to bed

3 go — to school

4 do — up

5 play — with friends

6 take — home

7 come — dressed

8 go — a shower

2 Look, read, and write questions and answers.

	⏰	👕	🏫	🏠	📖
👩					
👦					

1 What time does Diego get up?

He gets up at seven o'clock.

3 What time does Maria go to school?

_____

2 _____

He gets dressed at seven thirty.

4 _____

She comes home at two thirty.

Vocabulary Daily activities **Grammar** What time does he get dressed? He gets dressed at seven thirty.

5 Lesson 3

1 Look, read, and draw.

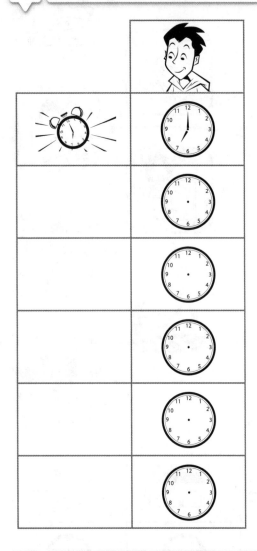

1 When do you get up?

I get up at seven o'clock in the morning.

2 When do you have breakfast?

I have breakfast at seven thirty in the morning.

3 When do you have lunch?

I have lunch at quarter to one in the afternoon.

4 When do you go home?

I go home at quarter past three in the afternoon.

5 When do you do your homework?

I do my homework at six thirty in the evening.

6 Max, when do you go to bed?

I go to bed at nine thirty in the evening.

2 Read and number in order. Answer for you.

☐ When do you go to bed?   ☐ When do you go home?

_____   _____

☐ When do you have lunch?   ☐ When do you have dinner?

_____   _____

☐ When do you have breakfast?   ☐ 1 When do you get up?

_____   _____

1 Look, read, and write.

sunrise   sunset   behind   ahead of

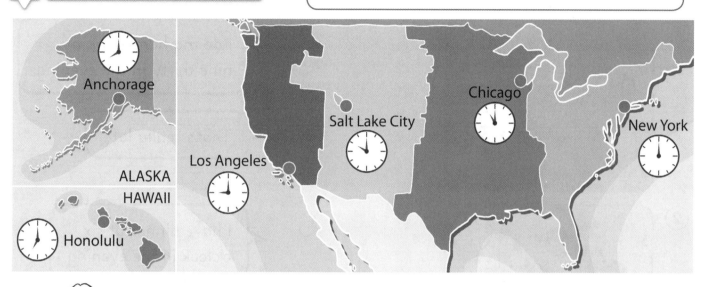

① I live in Honolulu. It's _____ here. I'm having breakfast.

② I live in Anchorage. Anchorage is _____ Honolulu.

③ I live in Los Angeles. Los Angeles is _____ New York.

④ I live in New York. It's twelve o'clock. There are seven hours before _____ .

2 Look at activity 1. Read and write.

1 In Chicago, it's nine o'clock in the morning. What time is it in New York?

_____

2 In New York, it's eleven o'clock. Is it sunrise or sunset in Anchorage?

_____

3 Is Salt Lake City ahead of or behind Honolulu?

_____

4 Is Chicago four hours or one hour behind New York?

_____

Vocabulary sunrise, behind, ahead of, sunset   35

5 | Lesson 5 | Everyday English!

1 Look, read, and match.

①

I do my homework at nine thirty in the evening.

That's really late!

②

I have dinner at six o'clock in the evening.

That's really early!

2 Look, read, and number in order.

①

- [ ] Hi Sam! Nice to meet you.
- [1] Rachel, this is Sam. He's new.
- [ ] Nice to meet you, too.

②

- [ ] I know! I have swimming club at six o'clock in the morning.
- [ ] That's really early!
- [ ] Yes! I get up at five o'clock in the morning.
- [ ] Are you tired?

5 Lesson 6

1 Look, read, and write.

twelve o'clock

early

Sunday

tired

late

Friday

Fernanda

From Monday to Friday, Fernanda gets up ¹ _____ at six thirty. She has breakfast and she goes to school at eight o'clock. She does her homework in the evening. On Saturday she goes to bed ² _____ .

On Saturday and ³ _____ , Yuto sleeps late. On Saturday, he gets up at ten o'clock in the morning. He has breakfast and he goes to basketball club. He plays basketball at ⁴ _____ . He plays with friends in the afternoon.

Yuto

Tom

From Monday to ⁵ _____ , Tom comes home from school at three thirty. He does his homework at four o'clock in the afternoon. He has dinner at six thirty. He goes to bed at eight thirty. He's ⁶ _____ !

2 Look at activity 1. Read and circle.

1 I go to school at eight o'clock.   Fernanda / Yuto / Tom

2 I do my homework at four o'clock.   Fernanda / Yuto / Tom

3 On Saturday, I go to bed late.   Fernanda / Yuto / Tom

4 On Saturday, I play basketball.   Fernanda / Yuto / Tom

5 On Monday, I have dinner at six thirty.   Fernanda / Yuto / Tom

6 Helping at Home

Lesson 1 | Story: Professor Green's Robots

1 Read and make a ✓ or an ✗.

①

I can see three robots. ☐

I can see Professor Green. ☐

I can see Lily. ☐

②

The robot is happy. ☐

The robot is sad. ☐

The robot is tired. ☐

③

The robot is talking. ☐

The robot is writing. ☐

Stella is listening. ☐

④

The robots are playing soccer. ☐

They are happy. ☐

Professor Green is sad. ☐

2 What chores do the robots do? Circle.

fold clothes   set the table   wash the dishes   make the bed   vacuum the carpet

6 Lesson 2

1 Look, read, and write. Draw a ☺ or a ☹ for you.

wash the dishes   make the bed   clean the bedroom   cook dinner

①  ☺

②  ☺

_____

③  ☺

④  ☺

_____

2 Look, read, and write about you.

do the laundry   lay the table   ~~vacuum the carpet~~   fold clothes
always   often   ~~sometimes~~   never

①

I sometimes vacuum the carpet.

②

_____

③

④

_____

1 Look, read, and match.

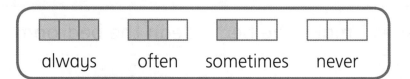

always   often   sometimes   never

①

②

③

④

● How often do you cut the grass?
I never cut the grass.

● How often do you water
the plants?
I often water the plants.

● How often do you take out
the trash?
I always take out the trash.

● How often do you walk the dog?
I sometimes walk the dog.

2 Look, read, and write.

	Amy	Tim
	☐☐☐	▨☐☐
	▨▨▨	▨▨☐
	▨☐☐	☐☐☐
	▨▨☐	▨▨▨

Amy

1 How often do you walk the dog?
 <u>I never walk the dog.</u>

2 How often do you cut the grass?
_____

Tim

3 How often do you take out the trash?
_____

4 How often do you water the plants?
_____

Vocabulary Outdoor chores **Grammar** How often do you walk the dog? I never walk the dog.

Lesson 4 **Social Studies**

1 Look, read, and match.

①  ②  ③  ④

wait for the light

walk on the sidewalk

wear bright clothes

use the crosswalk

2 Read and draw.

You can't cross before you look and listen.

Road Safety

 Always use the crosswalk.

You can't play on the road.

Always walk on the sidewalk.

You can't cross when the light is red.

Always wear bright clothes when you ride your bike.

1 Look, read, and write.

together   living room   Let's   mess

My _____ is a _____ !

_____ clean it _____ .

2 Look, read, and write the words in order.

①

of   Can   too?   course.   fun.
cook,   I   That   ~~looks~~   ~~Yes,~~

That looks _____ .

_____

Yes, _____ .

②

it   a   clean   kitchen   Let's
mess!   My   together.   is

_____

_____

6 Lesson 6

1 Read and complete the chart.

Interview with my family

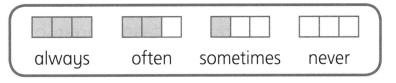

always   often   sometimes   never

Mom			☐☐☐		☐☐☐		☐☐☐	☐☐☐
Dad			☐☐☐	☐☐☐		☐☐☐		☐☐☐
Sally	☐☐☐	▨▨▨	☐☐☐	☐☐☐				
Josh		☐☐☐	☐☐☐		☐☐☐	☐☐☐		

Sally I always clean my bedroom. I love a clean bedroom! I never cook dinner, but I often wash the dishes. I sometimes take out the trash. But I don't like that.

Josh I sometimes cook dinner. I like chicken and rice for dinner. I always walk the dog. I love my dog! I often cut the grass. It's fun! I never clean my bedroom.

Mom I always vacuum the carpet. I often do the laundry. I never walk the dog because Josh always walks the dog. I often cook dinner. I like cooking!

Dad I sometimes cook dinner. I like roast beef and mashed potatoes for dinner. I always take out the trash and I sometimes do the laundry. I often cut the grass.

2 Write a question and answer for each person.

1 Sally, how often do you cook dinner? I never cook dinner.

2 _____ _____

3 _____ _____

4 _____ _____

Revision 3

1 Read and complete the chart.

cut the grass   ~~get up~~   have breakfast   cook dinner
make the bed   get dressed   go to bed   set the table
wash the dishes   walk the dog   take a shower   take out the trash

In the bedroom	In the kitchen or dining room	Outside	In the bathroom
get up			

2 Look, find, and circle.

h	a	v	e	a	s	n	a	c	k	e	p	c	h
d	z	f	o	c	o	v	m	r	z	t	l	l	v
n	c	f	d	x	o	x	g	j	t	w	a	e	a
x	t	o	o	s	a	s	i	h	d	a	y	a	c
f	b	l	h	b	v	h	d	m	d	t	w	n	u
n	x	d	o	b	e	p	q	h	o	e	i	t	u
f	d	c	m	f	q	r	m	y	t	r	t	h	m
o	b	l	e	m	e	o	y	w	h	t	h	e	t
t	k	o	w	o	d	t	f	u	e	h	f	b	h
g	o	t	o	s	c	h	o	o	l	e	r	e	e
h	m	h	r	k	t	s	b	e	a	p	i	d	c
u	u	e	k	y	c	u	c	w	u	l	e	r	a
b	b	s	h	v	i	r	t	q	n	a	n	o	r
p	y	w	g	j	n	q	y	l	d	n	d	o	p
c	o	m	e	h	o	m	e	f	r	t	s	m	e
g	x	z	a	x	f	i	u	r	y	s	h	t	t

3 Read, look, and write *H* for *Henry* or *D* for *Dad*.

My name's Henry and this is my dad. I get up at ⏰. I always make my bed in the morning. My dad gets up at ⏰. My dad goes to work at ⏰. I go to school at ⏰. I eat lunch at ⏰. My dad eats lunch at ⏰. I come home at ⏰. In the afternoon, I always walk the dog and I always do my homework. My dad comes home at ⏰. He often cooks dinner. We have dinner at ⏰. I go to bed at ⏰. In the evening, my dad often takes out the trash. He goes to bed at ⏰.

4 Look at Activity 1. Read and write.

1 What time does Henry go to school?   <u>He goes to school at seven o'clock.</u>

2 When do Henry and his dad have dinner?   They _____

3 How often does Henry make his bed?   He _____

4 How often does Henry's dad cook dinner? He _____

5 When does Henry do his homework?   He _____

At the Doctor's

1 Order the story. Read and circle.

These / Those are for you, Amy.

What beautiful flowers! Thank you!

These are the doctors. They help sick people. They're using the Internet.

1

How do you feel?

I have a toothache / stomach ache.

Do you have a fever?

Yes / No, I don't.

You have a **cold** / **cough**. Drink some water and go to bed.

Good morning, Amy. I'm Doctor Evans. How do you feel?

I have a sore **ear** / **throat** and a headache.

Oh, look! It's Amy!

Is / Are she sick?

Internet Doctors

Let's visit Amy.

FLOWERS

Look! A **book** / **flower** store. We can surprise her.

1 Look, read, and write. Find the hidden word.

①
②
③
④
⑤
⑥
⑦

cold   cough   fever   headache
earache   stomach ache   sore throat

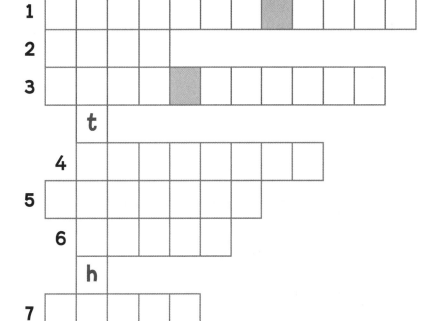

1
2
3 | | | | t |
4
5
6 | | | | h |
7

The hidden word is __ __ __ __ __ __ __ __ __

2 Unscramble the question and write the answers. Draw.

do How feel? you   _____

①

_____ a fever.

②

_____ a toothache.

7 **Lesson 3**

1 Look, read, and circle.

①

When I have a cough,
I **take medicine / go to the dentist.**

②

When I have a headache,
I **take medicine / stay in bed.**

③

When I have a toothache,
I **go to the doctor / go to the dentist.**

④

When I have a sore throat,
I **take medicine / go to the doctor.**

2 Look, read, and write.

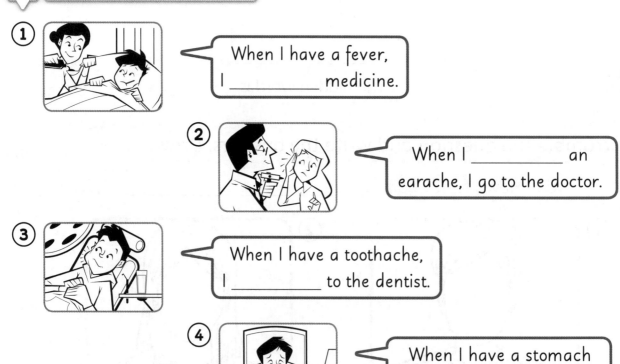

① When I have a fever,
I _____ medicine.

② When I _____ an
earache, I go to the doctor.

③ When I have a toothache,
I _____ to the dentist.

④ When I have a stomach
ache, I _____ in bed.

Vocabulary Remedies **Grammar** When I have a fever, I take medicine.

1 Look, read, and match.

salty

bitter

sour

sweet

2 Read and write.

 What's your favorite salty food?

_____

 What's your favorite sour food?

_____

 What's your favorite sweet food?

_____

 Think of a new ice cream flavor. What is it?

_____

 What food do you like and your friends don't like?

_____

 What foods do your parents like and you don't like?

_____

1 Look, read, and write.

I'm sorry. Get well soon!   I have a headache and a sore throat.
Thank you!   Hi! How do you feel?

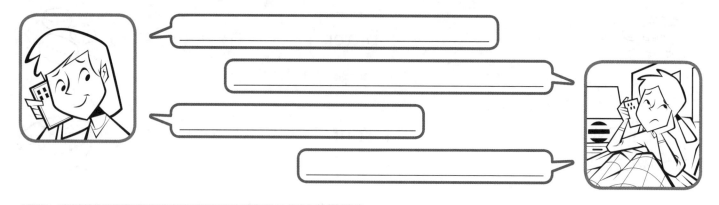

2 Look, read, and number in order.

Get well soon!

Thank you!

Which one do you want?

I want the big one, please.

How do you feel?

I have a cough and a sore throat.

When I have a cough, I take medicine.

1 Read and write.

> www.onlyphotos.com   www.musictobuy.com
> www.lovesoccer.com

Our Favorite Websites!

① Jasmin

I visit _____ when I want information about my favorite soccer team. I go there to read news about my favorite soccer players. I also like reading about their favorite foods, films, and music.

② Amir

I go to _____ to find new music. I always look at the website with my friends. You can listen to lots of music and buy the music you like.

③ Finn

I go to _____ to see my friend's pictures. I like to look at pictures of my friends' vacations. They're often interesting and sometimes they're funny. It's a great website because you can write a message under the picture.

2 Look at activity 1. Read and write.

1 Who writes a message on the website? _____

2 Who buys something on the website? _____

3 Who reads news on the website? _____

4 Who listens to something on the website? _____

5 Who looks at the website with their friends? _____

6 Who thinks something on the website is funny? _____

A Holiday Weekend

Lesson 1 | Johnny Sky's Vacation

1 Look, read, and write.

> I like going to the beach.   Let's go shopping.
> Let's go on a boat ride!   I like visiting a museum.
> What do you like doing on vacation?   Put these on.

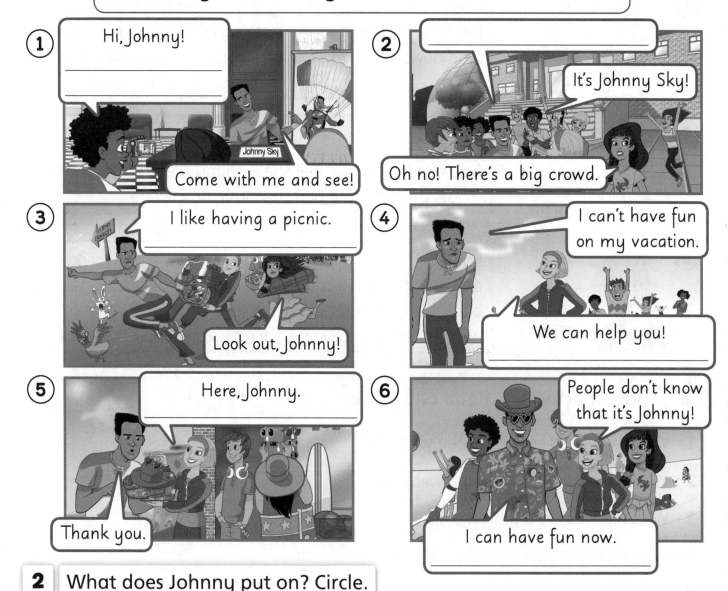

2 What does Johnny put on? Circle.

a hat   a belt   sunglasses   gloves

1 Read and write. Match.

> shopping   friends   to the movies   a museum
> a picnic   at a restaurant   on a boat ride   to the beach

1 go _____ ●

2 eat _____ ●

3 visit _____ ●

4 go _____ ●

5 go _____ ●

6 have _____ ●

7 meet _____ ●

8 go _____ ●

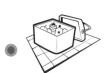

2 Look, read, and write. Draw.

¹ going	² boat ride	³ meeting	⁴ friends	⁵ I
⁶ on	⁷ visiting	⁸ like	⁹ the	¹⁰ afternoon
¹¹ museum	¹² a	¹³ morning	¹⁴ evening	¹⁵ In

What do you like doing on vacation?

① 15 9 13 5 8 7 12 11

<u>In the morning, I like</u> _____ .

② 15 9 10 5 8 1 6 12 2

_____

③ 15 9 14 5 8 3 4

_____

1 Look, read, and write.

| playing don't Do magazines you painting |
| do like No computer watching Yes |

① Do _____ like _____ TV?

Yes, I _____ .

② _____ you like _____ pictures?

_____ , I don't.

③ Do you like _____ _____ games?

_____ , I do.

④ Do you _____ reading _____?

No, I _____ .

2 Write the words in order to make questions. Answer for you.

1 painting you pictures? Do like

_____

_____

3 you Do watching TV? like

_____

_____

2 computer like games? Do you playing

_____

_____

4 magazines? reading you Do like

_____

_____

Vocabulary Indoor activities **Grammar** Do you like playing computer games? Yes, I do. / No, I don't.

1 Look, circle, and write.

thapmplasticbaghaercmfishinglineoipleoplmetalcanxfhuyzutplasticbottlefde

1 _____

2 _____

3 _____

4 _____

2 Read and complete the chart.

Beach Clean!

Come to a beach clean at Yellow Sands Beach!

Come and help make the beach clean! Sea animals eat plastic. It makes them sick. Metal cans can cut you. Fishing lines are dangerous for birds. Pick up litter and help birds and sea animals.

Bring gloves and a big bag for the trash.

Come with your friends and have fun!

It's on Saturday May 3rd at 3 o'clock in the afternoon.

Beach Clean				
Why?	Where?	When?	What time?	Bring?
Help birds and sea animals.	_____	_____	_____	_____
This is dangerous!		This isn't dangerous.		

1 Look, read, and circle.

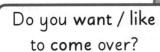

Do you **want** / like to come over?

This **morning** / afternoon. At five thirty.

Yes, please. / Thank you. When? / Why?

2 Look, read, and match.

①

I have a stomach ache.

Get well soon!

Thank you.

②

I like this pizza. Do you?

Yes, I like it a lot.

③

My bedroom is a mess.

Let's clean it up together.

④

Do you want to come over?

Yes, please! When?

After school.

1 **Read and number.**

1 Yes, I do. I like picnics on the beach!

2 It's great! It's very sunny here!

3 No, I don't. I think shopping is boring.

4 Yes, I do. When it's rainy, I like visiting museums. I like reading magazines, too.

5 I like going to the beach. I like playing volleyball at the beach!

John: Hi, Ana! How's your vacation?

Ana: 2

John: What do you like doing on vacation?

Ana: ☐

John: Great! Volleyball is fun! Do you like having picnics?

Ana: ☐

John: Do you like visiting museums?

Ana: ☐

John: Do you like going shopping?

Ana: ☐

John: Me, too. Well, have fun on vacation, Ana!

John

Ana

2 **Write three more questions about holiday activities. Ask a friend. Write their answers.**

Do you like eating at a restaurant?   Yes, I do.

_____   _____

_____   _____

_____   _____

Revision 4

1 Look, draw, and write.

①    _____ cold

②    _____

③     _____

④     _____

⑤    _____

⑥     _____

2 Complete the puzzle.

■	❀	◎	✻	✧	▲	◗	➤	▣	◆	✳	✳	◯	✛	☆	⬢	◻	✷	☉	✦	♥	◈	●	⬥	✳	★
a	b	c	d	e	f	g	h	i	j	k	l	m	n	o	p	q	r	s	t	u	v	w	x	y	z

① ✷✧☉✦■♥✷■✛✦
   eat at a __ __ __ __ __ __ __ __ __ __ __

② ❀✧■◎➤
   go to the __ __ __ __ __

③ ◯♥☉✧♥◯
   visit a __ __ __ __ __ __

④ ◯☆⬥▣✧☉
   go to the __ __ __ __ __ __

⑤ ⬢▣◎✛▣◎
   have a __ __ __ __ __ __

⑥ ☉➤☆●⬢▣✛◗
   go __ __ __ __ __ __ __ __

⑦ ❀☆■✦　✷▣✻✧
   go on a __ __ __ __ __　__ __ __ __

⑧ ▲✷▣✧✛✻☉
   meet __ __ __ __ __ __ __

3 Read and circle.

How do you **do / feel**?

I'm sick. I **have / get** a stomach ache

I'm sorry. When I have a stomach ache, I **take / go** to the doctor.

I like to **stay / go** in bed!

Have / Take medicine and **stay / get** well soon!

4 Read and write.

magazines   eating   going   like   What
doing   having   museums   painting

Dad: We want to take a vacation, Kate! What do you like ¹ _____ on vacation?

Kate: I like ² _____ to the beach. And I like ³ _____ a picnic.

Dad: Let's go to Italy! There are beautiful beaches in Italy! There are great museums, too. When it's rainy, I like going to ⁴ _____. Do you ⁵ _____ going to museums?

Kate: No, I don't. When it's rainy, I like reading ⁶ _____ and I like ⁷ _____ pictures.

Dad: You can paint pictures of Italy!

Kate: ⁸ _____ do you like doing on vacation, Dad?

Dad: I like ⁹ _____ in a restaurant. Italian food is great!

Olympic Games

1 Look, read, and write.

show   stadium   trophy   champion

①

②

③

④

_____   _____   _____   _____

2 Look at activity 1. Read and write.

At the Olympic Games, there are sportspeople from many different countries. Everyone wants to be the ¹_____ of their sport! There isn't a ²_____ but there is a medal for the champions.

At the start, there is an Opening Ceremony. It's in a big ³_____ . There's an Olympic flag and an Olympic torch. The Olympic torch is fire from Greece. Then, there's a big ⁴_____ with music, dancing, and fireworks!

3 Read and circle.

1 At the Olympic Games, is there a trophy? **Yes, there is. / No, there isn't.**

2 Are there people from lots of countries? **Yes, there are. / No, they aren't.**

3 Is the Olympic Stadium big or small? **It's big. / It's small.**

4 Where is the Olympic torch from? **Egypt. / Greece.**

5 Are there fireworks at the show? **Yes, there are. / No, there aren't.**

What Money Can Buy

1 Look, read, and match.

one cent   bills   coins   dollar

2 Read and write.

Zahra

    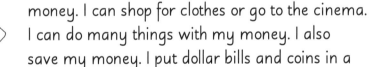

Every week, my parents give me some money. It's good because I can shop for presents. Or when I go to a cafe with my friends, I can use my money. I can shop for clothes or go to the cinema. I can do many things with my money. I also save my money. I put dollar bills and coins in a jar every week. I want to buy a new skateboard. I have 56 dollars and 95 cents now! I need 72 dollars to buy my skateboard. I'm very excited!

1 What does Zahra do with her money? _____

2 Where does she save her money? _____

3 What does she want to buy? _____

4 How much money does she have? _____

5 How much money does she need? _____

1 Look, read, and write.

cowboy   ranch   calf   busy

①

②

③

④

_____   _____   _____   _____

2 Read and number in order.

Johnny is a cowboy. He lives on a ranch. He gets up at five o'clock in the morning! He takes the cows to the grass. At five thirty, he takes breakfast to the horses. Then he rides his horse for two hours. His horse is called "Flame." He comes home to the ranch at eight o'clock. He has breakfast at eight thirty. He's very busy in the morning. He has lunch at two o'clock in the afternoon. In the evening, he takes the horses and the cows inside. He goes to bed at nine thirty. He's tired and happy!

He comes home to the ranch. ☐   He has breakfast. ☐

He gets up. 1   He takes the horses and cows inside. ☐

He goes to bed. ☐   He rides his horse. ☐

He takes breakfast to the horses. ☐   He has lunch. ☐

Vocabulary cowboy, ranch, calf, busy

Coney Island

1 Look, read, and match.

 ①  ②  ③  ④

rollercoaster   ride   theme park   exciting

2 Read and circle *True* or *False*.

Coney Island is in New York, in the USA. People go there to have fun! You can go on rides in the summer, but not in the winter. On Friday evenings, there are fireworks. There's a beach at Coney Island, too. You can swim and play volleyball.

There are many restaurants. There's also a stadium! You can watch baseball there. There's a famous roller coaster. It's called "The Cyclone" and it's almost one hundred years old! Coney Island is a great place to go on vacation!

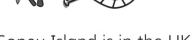  

1	Coney Island is in the UK.	True / False
2	You can go on rides in the winter.	True / False
3	There are fireworks on Friday evenings.	True / False
4	You can play volleyball at Coney Island beach.	True / False
5	You can watch baseball at a stadium on Coney Island.	True / False
6	There's a famous roller coaster called "The Storm."	True / False

OXFORD
UNIVERSITY PRESS

Great Clarendon Street, Oxford, OX2 6DP, United Kingdom

Oxford University Press is a department of the University of Oxford.
It furthers the University's objective of excellence in research, scholarship,
and education by publishing worldwide. Oxford is a registered trade
mark of Oxford University Press in the UK and in certain other countries

ISBN: 978 0 19 403367 1

Printed in China

This book is printed on paper from certified and well-managed sources

ACKNOWLEDGEMENTS

Back cover photograph: Oxford University Press building/David Fisher

Cover Image: Graham Alder/MM Studios

Illustrations by: Tony Forbes pp. 2 (calendars), 7 (orchestra), 8 (children playing
guitar), 9, 14 (children in camp site), 15, 16 (Spanish flag, child's drawing),
17, 22 (children playing videogames), 27, 28 (children choosing skateboards),
31 (supermarket conveyor belt), 33 (getting up, going to school, studying,
going home), 36 (children at school), 37 (clock, calendars and children),
42 (children in living room), 44 (school bus, snack and playing), 47 (cold,
headache and cough), 51, 53 (bag, friends chatting and boat), 55 (ex. 1), 56
(girls), 59 (family), 60 (stadium, podium, trophy and show), 61, 62 (calf, ranch,
cowboy and people in ranch), 63 (ex. 1); Bill Greenhead/Illustration pp. 3, 4,
10, 18, 24, 32, 38, 46, 52; Andrew Painter pp. 2 (characters), 5, 6, 11 (children
with flags), 12, 13 (monuments), 16 (all items except Spanish flag), 19, 20, 21,
23, 25, 26 (pencils, table with potatoes, eggs and flowers on), 30, 33 (playing,
yawning, bathing, getting dressed, clock, clothes, school, house books), 34, 37
(Fernanda, Yuto and Tom), 39, 40, 41 (ex. 1), 43, 44 (lamp and books, cleaning,
watering plants, doing the laundry, house, vacuuming and folding clothes),
47 (stomachache, sore throat, earache and fever), 48, 49 (ex. 2), 50 (girls on the
phone), 53 (menu, picnic basket, movie tickets, sunhat, sunscreen and leaflet),
54, 57, 58; Lorenzo Sabbatini/The Organisation pp. 7 (children talking),
8 (children doing sports), 14 (children playing table tennis), 22 (children
shopping), 28 (girl choosing school bag), 29, 31 (characters), 33 (characters),
35, 36 (children talking), 41 (ex. 2), 42 (children in kitchen), 45, 47 (neutral
face), 50 (story), 56 (children on the phone), 59 (children on the phone), 60
(objects around text), 62 (cowboy in ranch and objects around text); Fred Van
Deelen pp. 11 (hotel), 13 (Australian and Mexican monuments), 26 (potatoes,
olives and balloons), 49 (ex. 1), 55 (ex. 2), 63 (ex. 2).

*The publishers would like to thank the following for permission to reproduce photographs
and other copyright material*: Dennis Kitchen Studio, Inc. p. 61 (one dollar bill);
Shutterstock p. 61 (stacks of US dollars/lendy16, one dollar coins falling/
serg_dibrova, American cent coin/Sascha Burkard)